Riding Thermals to Winter Grounds

Critical Praise for the books of Djelloul Marbrook

Artemisia's Wolf (title story, *A Warding Circle*)

...successfully blends humor and satire (and perhaps even a touch of magic realism) into its short length...an engrossing story, but what might strike the reader most throughout the book is its infusion of breathtaking poetry...a stunning rebuke to notoriously misogynist subcultures like the New York art scene, showing us just how hard it is for a young woman to be judged on her creative talent alone.

—Tommy Zurhellen, *Hudson River Valley Review*

Saraceno

...Djelloul Marbrook writes dialogue that not only entertains with an intoxicating clickety-clack, but also packs a truth about low-life mob culture *The Sopranos* only hints at. You can practically smell the anisette and filling-station coffee.

—Dan Baum, author of *Gun Guys* (2013), *Nine Lives: Mystery, Magic, Death and Life in New Orleans* (2009) and others

...a good ear for crackling dialogue... I love Marbrook's crude, raw music of the streets. The notes are authentic and on target...

—Sam Coale, *The Providence (RI) Journal*

...an entirely new variety of gangster tale... a Mafia story sculpted with the most refined of sensibilities from the clay of high art and philosophy...the kind of writer I take real pleasure in discovering...a mature artist whose rich body of work is finally coming to light.

—Brent Robison, editor, *Prima Materia*

Far from Algiers

...as succinct as most stanzas by Dickinson... an unusually mature, confidently composed first poetry collection.

—Susanna Roxman (author of *Crossing the North Sea*) in *Prairie Schooner*

...brings together the energy of a young poet with the wisdom of long experience.

—Edward Hirsch, Guggenheim Foundation

Brushstrokes and Glances

Whether it is commentary on state power, corporate greed, or the intensely personal death of a loved one, Djelloul Marbrook is clear sighted, eloquent, and precise. As the title of the collection suggests, he uses the lightest touch, a collection of fragments, brushstrokes and glances, to fashion poems that resonate with truth and honesty.

—Phil Constable, *New York Journal of Books*

Riding Thermals to Winter Grounds

poems by
Djelloul Marbrook

LEAKY BOOT PRESS

Riding Thermals to Winter Grounds
by Djelloul Marbrook

Acknowledgments

"Hospital earth" first appeared in *Writing for Peace*, April 7, 2015.
"Presumption of dandelions" first appeared in *Vox Populi* (2015).

First published in 2017 by
Leaky Boot Press
http://www.leakyboot.com

Copyright © 2017 Djelloul Marbrook
All rights reserved

No part of this book may be reproduced or transmitted in any form or by any means, electronic, mechanical, photocopying, recording, or otherwise, without prior written permission of the author.

ISBN: 978-1-909849-27-3

Sell your cleverness and buy bewilderment.
—Jalal-ud-Din Mohamed Rumi

*...In this bewilderness
we must love what we deny.*
—"Bewilderness," *Riding thermals to winter grounds*

For Hart Crane (1899-1932), who said—

One must be drenched in words, literally soaked in them, to have the right ones form themselves into the proper patterns at the right moment.

Contents

Riding thermals to winter grounds

Riding thermals to winter grounds	15
Bearings	16
Twelve-mile limit	18
Forests hurtling	19
Ghostedness	21
Serpent goddess	23
Speck	24
Whoa goddam	25
Making enemies	26
Whale of a man	28
Flourish of lies	29
Famine	30
Distillates & decoctions	31
Hard of hearing	33
My brain picks up its sticks	34
Stars align and gutter	36
Dumb shit's day	38
Elixir of the ordinary	39
That something	41

Jongleurs of sobs

The windings	45
Ember	46
Jongleurs of sobs	47
Hatshepsut would miss me	48
Mired in chaos	51
Up in the castle	52

Lilacs	53
To cut away	54
Putting on my socks	55
A born IED	56
Double agents	57
Words, do not trust the page	58
Grateful for oafs	59
Walking slow without a bit of pain	60
Hooyiyay	61
Had we pursued	62
What Luciano said	63
Skirt disappearing behind a door	64
The death of me to say	65

Deuteronomy 23:2

Deuteronomy 23:2	69
No berserker in its maze	70
Which butterfly	71
Dancing the pale	72
Hurt	73
Diet of whales	74
Presumption of dandelions	75
Death-dancing	76
Watching the furies slip by	77
Was it a dream?	78
Wary greetings	79
Not since Brooklyn	80
Dragons kinder	81
Other sleeplessness to do	82
The drowning	83
What I'm doing in this room	84
Savage in your compassion	85
Jerusalem	86
Black hole	87
Waters rising	88
Gentrification	89
Eleven lines	90

Beyond Montauk

Without the fuss and bother of giving a damn	93
If you can't bring yourself	95
To make crows laugh	96
The painting	97
Bewilderness	98
Hospital earth	99
Witch's skirt	101
As if Hopper	102
Bird-watching	103
To hang on the doorknob	104
Sorting	105
Burnt stick	106
What more had I forgotten?	107
Letter to name withheld	108
I would like to wake in a formal garden	109
Beyond Montauk	110

Dumping the apartment

Dumping the apartment	113

Riding thermals to winter grounds

Riding thermals to winter grounds

Do I need these prescriptions to endure
the loudmouths & exhibitionists of the world?
They're not bell buoys or lighthouses,
so when does solitude turn to loneliness?
If I have to choose may I go back a way
to reconsider the curtain moving in the window
& the gray parents whose fumbling inside
led to my urgent mistake, a life
of unwantedness, a misdemeanor,
lewd and lascivious to the puritan,
hot & bothersome to a clean-up man
like me, a night janitor, a citizen
of Discordia in distress, fixing
to ride thermals to his winter grounds,
to go home. Turn off the radio,
lock the doors, put the trash in the street;
the fair means to Montauk
grow out of my shoulder blades.

Bearings

I
Faces that threaten to disappear,
promise, threaten, seem likely
to disappear, are Lenten roses;
I am the snow they drink.
Nothing can be done for them
but adoration and resolve
not to gather them in love
or fear.
                    Who is the poison,
seer or seen, the pale rose
or one who leaves footprints
in the snow?
                    I looked back
as a child and noticed
I left no footprints anywhere.
How was I to honor that? How
to treat such faces as I met
as if I understood their right
to not accept the here and there
we use to get our bearings?

II
Who did you ever really like?
When all your going on
and all the goings on
subsided

did you show yourself
to anyone?
                      I think if you had
there would have been so little left
we might not have noticed you at all.
As it is you have been like
ink hanging in the air,
a fume
through which it's dangerous to walk.

There's no help for any of this
except our tendency to rot,
our insistence on being not.

Twelve-mile limit

Back up here and go to hell
in this little alleyway
that was your name.
Let the street return
to Giorgio di Chirico.
Be gone, popsicle in hand,
shoes untied, questions
spinning in the gutter
after rain.
          Where'd he go?
I dunno. Wasn't looking,
didn't care.
Coney Island maybe
or way out beyond Montauk
and the 12-mile limit
of what passes for living.
I dunno. He was in a hurry,
didn't leave his name.
But did he take it with him?
Who wants to know?
When the folding door of indifference fell
a blue skateboarder passed by
intent on midges as a dragonfly.

Forests hurtling

Think of what to think
when the bridges of the chasms of your mind
wash out and forests hurtle
to the sea bearing houses
where your memories live. Think
of how to think when time gives way
to the nonsense of a book
in which words do penance
and go to disappear because silence is annoyed
and canvas shakes off paint.

Think how you must feel
or is the point that you need not
feel or complain or approve
because you are fiber and thread
and all else is applied,
a kind of treatment,
an interpretation
of what is already satisfied?

Think of what to think
to slide to sleep
and not awake old quarrels
with other passengers
on this express of meteors.

Think of what not to know
until you fall asleep
and, falling, lose

all hope of getting
from one moment to the next,
and if that's not Nirvana
it will do for a sailor
as ecstatic as you.

Ghostedness

We, not in any royal sense,
but in memory of the child
who did not get out alive
left in a privet chapel
to be eaten by caretakers,
left without a name.

> What bedroom is safe
> after such savagery?

We are four-footed,
we kick up bones,
endure too much,
forget too little,
love ghostedness.

Nothing is lost, all is found
transformed, its true face
unbearable, and therefore
two must go where one
would have been lost,
two hand in hand
in what shrinks would call
an illness, not a split
but a loyalty dogs would understand.

> Are we naked not to have a name,
> or bearable, equipped
> to cross the field of fire
> air-conditioned and alive?

My painted side is like
a mirror's silver, working,
its hieroglyphs a shipper's label,
the history of how
it got here and not there,
a provenance of no concern
to my enemies, therefore
their undoing. I reflect
the boy you can't see.

Serpent goddess

On a rock ledge the slitherer suns.
The booted hiker may survive her,
Kindle flashing in her hand:
but she is herself the lone survivor
of a cataclysmic embitterment,
the estrangement of her birth.
She is more seen to be going,
vanishing under rocks and leaves,
than coming to our bloodletting.
The venom of her tooth is despair
so pure there is no antidote.
Even the eagle riding a thermal
is not eager to clutch her. That
is as much as it knows of consequence,
much more than the hiker knows
with her aspirations and sweat.
Only men attack what they can't swallow.
Society becomes their indigestion.
What if the hiker salutes and swings away,
wiser even than the eagle?
It would beg a reordering of heaven
to earn such a blessing merely
by hallowing a little discretion.

Speck

Forever is a very short time,
a speck caught in a viewing scope
signalling the eye to send
distorted images to the brain,
to imply whatever's wanted
will never come, therefore
there's plenty of time to dicker
wth what's going on, thinking
looking back's for someone else
and you will die gloriously,
being spared of retrospect.
Forever blew up in the face
of an old man in a mirror, who can't
remember what he was waiting for.
Verbs continue to serve him well,
but adverbs seem equivocal,
adjectives foul, and the only pronoun
of any use is you lugging
that very short time around.

Whoa goddam

Goddam itchy earwax
full of sirens and alarms,
goddam dandelion rheum
making streetlights bloom,
but if I rubbed you all away
would anything make sense?

Wouldn't I have to start again,
learn to tie my shoes,
commit what crimes in my head
to interrupt the tedium
of pretending I don't know
what I know so goddam well?

Making enemies

It's not like that any more,
as if I ever knew what that was like.

I think I mean my life,
but what I remember of it
is shifty, nothing I'd believe
if I were listening to it.

Like that, that what? Ceres?

Some life I still smelled of
when I began making enemies,
my job if I was to walk straight
and not slink?

And as for talk,
well, here I am, running out of breath.

I think it's not like this any more,
this skating on the moaning plates
of resentment and overture
to some power that ought to be.

I'm for the horror of the place,
this that that feels like a home
over there against the wall
splattered with the brains
of the dumb-ass bullies I knew.

We survived each other only
to be walled in by ourselves,

persistent, exhausted selves
we're unable to shake,
the very wheels of going on,
and if I lost one of those wheels
some asshole would volunteer,
out of the closet sniggering,
reminding me of what I blew,
offering me a hand.

What was it like then,
half past the summer of when?

Like having parents who lived in the walls
and not being their pleasure
but rather a probationary guest.

I was desperate to get past the pronouns
and the brackets and parentheses of time,
desperate to distrust being here now,
there not being anywhere to go.

And when it began to rain
I wasn't desperate for the sun.

This when, was it a birthmark
borne from a savage place
and hidden in my other shape,
the one that shimmers freely
for the most desperate, then
subsides before the wardens
enter the room—half past
the summer when I dreamed
that all I had to do was ask
and love would be given me
like starlight reaching me
and I would bathe in it
to be somehow cleansed of this
that weighs and wears me down,
this doubtfulness?

Whale of a man

He blows to breathe, but only in front of shop windows,
his breach an epiphany five stories high, a twist
and a squall before our thresholds, and this harpoon
is my determination to understand: does he yearn
to fly or is this ecstatic somersault, this I-know-I-am
a consternation so profound it makes Ahab envious
of such gnosis in Behemoth that we would rather drown
than be incapable of it? Would this old man be amused
that I think him a cetacean? No human looks as baleful
a witness that hope's a dread idea. He has no ideas.
His purpose is to snort impediments away, to breathe
what waits to be sensed, to sniff one moment's scent.

Flourish of lies

They wore their schadenfreude so stylishly,
is that why I remember them? A neurologist
would talk of short-term memory loss,
how older memories hang on doorknobs
and overstay their welcome, but I choose
to think the ones I would like to remember
are happy to let me go, to exact nothing
for the pleasure of their company, and so
I claim of aging that it's discretion
and of the lies that flourish in faces,
I'm perfectly willing to water them
and not behead them with lawnmowers
of dissatisfaction. Each face is a garden
in a certain state of decay; in that decay
the future is born and joy leans towards the sun.

Famine

I've kicked my ass all over the world
for sipping poisons like an oenologist,
but it's not without its rewards:
the cracks in buildings speak
and I'm the plenipotentiary
of a foreign power whose name I forget.
I enjoy name recognition
among the ghosts of certain places
because they recognize a fellow taster,
one who let the invaders settle in
before levying a dhimmi tax on them.
This is my Islam, that I died
so often standing up, stepping out
to get a breath of air and going in
for all that crap about genetics;
my Islam is noticing what's going on,
burning the authorized version in oil drums
under bridges, growing abutments
to support my Queensboros
over rivers of shifting wrecks
& vortices of forgiveness not so much
as a famine of the eye.

Distillates & decoctions

Hear the painting, see the song,
extract of exaltation, concentrate
of awry and askance in the foot,
feeling like a bone spur, burning
like reflux, a synesthesiac loose
in a cosmos of commodities,
messing things up gloriously,
celebrating beliefs as kindling,
high on & exulting in disorder.

The grapes of wrath are stored
in the heel of my left foot, I gag
on overseasoned ideas and hope
to starve opprobriums I've been fed.
Distillates and decoctions
of things seen too well stoppered
in brown bottles hold out the promise
of an eventual cure, but where
would be the fun of chaos then?

There was no medicine for it,
not even Christian Science,
for my getting things so wrong,
for sniffing the underwear of things
and spotting the smirk of true intent;
in time I thought to hell with them
in their dressy righteousness. I saw

they would do anything to avert,
to divert my gaze, to shut my mouth.

Anything. I am not that profane.

Hard of hearing

I don't know what people are saying anymore.
My bad hearing's an excuse to make demands
on words only a medical examiner would make,
to leave a rough-sewn Y on their chests, to draw
conclusions the living twist themselves to evade.
What're they saying, these puppets on a string?
Why do regional accents that once I understood
fall off the map of comprehension now, and why
am I more than pleased to see words fly away,
having shitted in our coffee and hissed like geese?
And then there's the question of which one I'm talking to,
not then but now. Who are you that I imagine
you know what I'm saying? Take the name-droppers,
why drop them on me? Names are heavy burdens,
luggage best lost in airports, money manufactured
by bankrupt society. I'd rather flood with counterfeits
the makers of such currencies. Perhaps, perhaps
that's what I'm doing, holding words to impossible light.

My brain picks up its sticks

My brain has become an enigma machine;
I hope it's working for a decent state.
It scrambles whatever my ears send it,
it Photoshops the witness of my eyes.
It's a kind of blossom, strange fruit.
It turns the tide of words, it plays with them,
and when I make inquiries it says,
sit up straight, breathe slowly, exhale
as if you won't miss a damned thing, as if
the goddess you would have chosen chose
to inhabit you and you don't need to be you
anymore but rather that someone else
you've been talking to all these years,
that trustworthy wraith who has always held
your left hand as you cross a perilous strait.
I don't know what it's doing with the words
it's lifting off the pages of my mind, making
marvelous insects of them to bite sleepers
in their travels through their mishaps,
but I know it's about to rip the pages out
and make paper boats of them and then
what will there be left of me but my old
left-handedness once bullied out of me
and now returned like King Richard from
a crusade bearing mysterious riches
to bother a barely civilized land? Yes,

I'm content to let the machine subvert
and I thought I knew because for all I know
it is deposing the doppelganger of my life.

Stars align and gutter

My ass mumbles over macadam
as redbuds tumble by,
a kind of fellatio
squeezing old abuses out of me,

my ass unappeased by
the stories of my eyes,
road a wound opening, artery cut
in the body of a friend.

Hurtling ass dead reckoning
from ought to fraught
with fear of going nowhere
veering, not wheeling, like a crow.

Goddamn the presumption
distances must be closed
when I'd be all for staying
fondling glimpses of abandon

as if I had an invitation.
But my ass is sore and sorry
if unapologetic and it hurries
as if destination is irrelevant.

Is there a place to go,
some remembered orgasm
where stars align and gutter
in the plosives of my death?

A place where I might say
I saw something once,
I testified, and now I've come
to rest in once familiar arms?

Dumb shit's day

Get the dumb shit's foot soak,
hear him say outrageous things,
but not until he's had his sparkling water,
not until the day comes down to this,
off its high pretensions, pretty faces,
smirking help, hauteur of passersby,
and one smile that by all accounts
should not have been wasted on him,
but it was, and for that reason only
a wrong day cobbled itself together
over a pot of tea and an oatmeal cookie.

The tall man with a hair knot and a blazing face
smudged the uptown gloom with light,
downtown the granite face of a tall girl
stopped the sun in its leaky delirium
and saved a tinder forest across the river
while the dumb shit noticed all of this,
extrapolated a thing or two, and decided
that by no means anyone he encountered
deserved to know these done-with truths,
not being certifiably mad enough,
and so he would save them for a fellow fool.

Elixir of the ordinary

To see the wont of objects
—power, speech and vision—
break the hard illusion
of possessing anything at all,
resign from societies,
quit ideologies;
drift as fume
between shadows,
something akin to scent,
barely imaginable.

Nothing is accident;
that is to celebrate
elixir of the ordinary,
to hardly need to eat,
to see the undersides
of purposes
and surfaces,
to let objects speak
but never trade in words.

Can we do it,
can it be done,
can we consent
to let elements become
what a first glance
suggests to them,
what they suggest to us,

or must all be struggle
and squalid compromise?

That something

Ponds and fires and eyes of others, stare
one foot at a time, clothes dropping away
until the pretense of having been leaves
a burnt imprint on the grass, a stain
on the sidewalk, a few mysterious cuttings,
a shadow that cannot be accounted for.
That something in you that scared bullies
goes to rest in the one true nakedness—
you've given up fond places before
to stare into the eyes of others; the difference
is now you feel invisibility coming on,
a nakedness for which there is no cure,
a final illness for which your life has been
nostalgia, a condition for which there is no protocol.
It's what you get for such a life unblinking,
for climbing over the slanted girders of I
to get at the emplacements of them & finally
in torrents to pour from the clitoral cup of you
all over the black marble sheet of the earth.

Jongleurs of sobs

The windings

Everyone is a mirror
of the mind in which we exult.
Everything is a mirror
in which we see our purpose.
We are light refracted,
colors of an unknown god
poured through the pinholes
of the windings of religion.
We are an ecstasy of witness,
rogue operatives at work
undermining belief.

Ember

Life is a crisis, a cry
to go back into what
that exploded
& went its way
leaving an ember
on the pavement
of another galaxy
& then it rained.

Jongleurs of sobs

Families re-form, strangers group,
cake is left for sparrows.
Witness this re-panic:
words leave their meanings behind

in search of melodies
from other planets, meanings
find new utterances
beribboning our nakedness.

Shape is whimsy, dogma flummox,
and in a sea of arabesques
we set sail as numerals
drunk on uncertainties.

The lame begin to dance.
Grave means gravityless.
Jongleurs of sobs,
we flow through walls.

Hatshepsut would miss me

I curled up in a krater encircled by eidolons
and dreamed of three exquisite behinds
while Hadrian smiled across the courtyard.

My long conversation with Charles Cloypel
had exhausted me, I left Don Quixote
in his care and discussed with Caravaggio
the lute's indebtedness to the oud.

It snowed outside and people stank
of their disguises and hangups. Caligula
in particular complained of the cameras,
but Marcus Aurelius silenced him
with a stare. Hatshepsut would miss me.
She was really the only one whose anger
I feared, but it was a long day and I was tired,
and I didn't want to deal with the cats.

You know me as a probe of light, a glare,
something darting in the corner of your eye,
or perhaps that thing you should have ignored.

Seduce me to pixels and archival rest,
resurrect me as solvent intent
on cleaning up history and tormenting
the eye stuck open before grandeur.
I am studying you after a good night's sleep
which is all I ever wanted to do
when I had to wear clothes and speak,

studying you from the classical orders,
Doric, Corinthian and Ionic, applauding
the rebellion of your elements searching
for elixirs. I am beckoning you to them—
over here, between Artemis's toes, there in Daphne's cleft—
but your grand compulsion to be seen
is misleading you, and in my despair
I catch my breath in Ville d'Avray or tryst
with Aphrodite in the rigging of Turner's ships.

I have alternatives, you have none unless
you're wondering while you're leaving
why Renoir's dancer is looking
over her partner's shoulder at you.
My to-do list is longer than the janitors',
longer than the acquisitions department's:
I will sail navels of goddesses in coracles of dust,
I will paint their nipples with sunsets.

This is the heaven of the five-year-old boy
standing across Eastern Parkway
worrying if the shabtis in the Brooklyn Museum
have enough to eat, a dream edited and redacted only once—
he dared to ship the dream to the Metropolitan.
He liked its grand stairways and most of all
its Hadrian, sad, amused, haunted by Antinous.

Never mind which grime, which solvent,
we are all shape-shifters held up by our pretenses.
Never mind which lost glove or tear shed
on Pharoah's pedestal, never mind
the grand ambitions and compulsions
we force ourselves to entertain, we are dust,
particulates put together for a time
and we ought to be happy to dissolve
to make marble shine, to refract light,
happy our contraptions did not last.

I don't know how I came by this heaven
except that I rehearsed. Is that right
or is it that I loved the idea of loving art
so fiercely that I became that elixir
my elements had been looking for
and so I came to where I belonged,
there being nothing, nothing reasonable to do?
I became worshipful dust and solvent,
forensic proof of someone's loneliness.

I became everything I had ever seen
in strangers' eyes. Never mind, never mind
what I said, it was lost in the o of the word.
I hear it rattling. Never mind, it was a distraction.
I am here now, under the mattes of prints,
a glint in a bolt of sun, a scent
description defiles, a consent to disappear.

Who are you, who was I but borrowed beings,
facsimiles until love leads us permanently
astray and we rejoin the welkin flowing?

Mired in chaos

You don't seem quite yourself.
Have you one to return to,
a proper inhabitant
known to the locals, accepted
and suspected of the usual
voyeurism, gossip, venality?
Or has that self accustomed
to unbelonging, especially
in cemeteries and places
where the illusion of repose
suggests foolish headlines
such as "mired in chaos"
and disrespect for words
becomes a fatal cockiness,
presumption we can operate
behind our own backs
pretending to a belonging
that ends up making strange?
There's a breathlessness to life
and all we hold dear belies
we're outside looking in
the fires of pretense.

Up in the castle

Sometimes we get in somebody's head
and the Marquis de Sade happens there.
In the worst of us there's some poor maid
helpless in the wine cellar of the castellan
and we see that our salvation is sucking up
or killing him, but then we wake up
and what was so clear last night dissolves
in the bright dishonest morning light.
On to the gas station and Starbucks,
never mind that in a moment of clarity
everything we trusted leered and we
understood that every day is a choice
and the sun does not go down in defeat.

Lilacs

Lilacs sell no indulgences.
They look better in a jar
than a vase, like moonshine.
Allow me to be drunk on you,
we say, needing permission.
Lilacs make everything all right,
not like doctors or lotteries,
like inaccessible priestesses
sailing on ecstasies
to trade in spices and mysteries.
A life is well lived if only
to have been touched by them.

To cut away

They're not where we left them,
we're not where they left us;
all that's left is a sob.
We couldn't wait, couldn't shake
our fear we own nothing
but are dying pretending we do.
Our delusion is to cut away
a part from the whole. If we could
we'd die, but we can't
no matter how grand the opera,
and that's why winning & losing
are the trompe l'oeils of fools.
They're not where we left them
but they're where they belong.
No one is ever parted.

Putting on my socks

Now putting on my socks is almost as hard
as recognizing my mother was not seven feet tall,
and gripping the creaky railing feels
like bracing for another day

The paint the Etruscans used is still drying
in the back rooms of my mind   The Arabs
are still experimenting with the lateen rig
and I am just beginning to remember I was born

convinced no one had done the math
and I had come to pay hell for a mistake
that could have been avoided were it not
for my love of silence

A born IED

Tell her what not to juxtapose,
invite her to lunch at the Carlisle,
it's your duty as patron of the arts.
Be motherly, be Modthrythly,
no, not lactatious but austere
as if her Dadaist itch were inappropriate.
But don't overdo, don't imply it smells bad.
The purpose is to inspire her to derange
whatever smacks of perfect logic.

Look as if you need to be juxtaposed,
as if it happened to you once,
something embarrassingly moist,
and this mad girl must be saved,
rescued from the sensible fools
who finance museums with junk bonds
and derivatives. Appeal to her whatnots
to bring down the house, any house,
to expose the itty-bitties all dolled up
as critical hauteur. She's a born IED,
and there's nothing she won't juxtapose
with the next improbability that comes off.

Double agents

Depends which way a mouth is pointing
whether a brain lets words in:
words have their own magnetic north,
double-agents in service
to their own gods, so watch
the triangulation of a mouth
and the way it shapes intent
because all words shift shape
and sail their own currents
no matter which way mind blows.

Words, do not trust the page

to protect them from predators.
They see themselves as naked slaves
in a cruel marketplace.
I do not blame them
and confess to be their enemy.
They want to be bonfires
or at least to do their part.
We gather for separate purposes
wanting warmth more than light,
and words do not like
our preferences. In our huddling and our wars
we do not notice them abandoning
their posts and going over
to the enemy only they have known about,
the terrible loss of having to speak,
the primativist instinct
that compels us to enslave
and write endless white papers
absolving us
from the hideous sin
of shackling them to the page.

Grateful for oafs

Almost as if we were welcome here
we avoid the glances of doormen and cops
and pretend not to notice the awry detail of things.

Each yellow cab reminds us that at a certain intersection
between the foofaraw of arriving here and settling in
we noticed we were regarded as dicey

and would always have to be ready to show our papers
to some officious oaf who, pray God, would think
they were in order and let us pass

to wherever we might be going.
How lucky we have been to find so many oafs,
but today, in our old age, we find it hard to breathe the acrid air.

Walking slow without a bit of pain

Some place where I have to be
(I haven't found it yet)
calls with sexual urgency,
a higher mathematics,
a calling similar to algebra,
a conjuring, a joining,
conjugal, which if pursued
destroys the personalities
I put on to conform.

This is surely how I become myself,
walking slowly, taking in
malpropositions and malapropisms,
hideous adaptations of the self
now hung in secondhand shops.
Not restored furniture,
not this bumfooted explorer,
I'm hot for what I was before
I forgot and settled down in despair.

Hooyiyay

Your aura is too big for this room.
Promise you'll never come here again
and I'll make it up to you in the alley
between the main drag and consequence.
I'll scrub the walls free of you
and wash my hands in the steaming piss
of our secret negotiations.
No one shall know of this heroic act
but our invisible throngs
singing hooyiyay in the creases of our bodies
to the rafters of the rescued place.
I saw your trouble getting through the door,
that tragic largeness of your seeming self,
and I acted like Jesus Christ to save
artifacts from horned apocalypse
by a certain tawdriness you understood
to be the necessary sacrifice. I write
this letter now to remind you
what I told you about washing your hands
when you remember me lest
they blind your eyes with the vinegar of regret.

Had we pursued

For what a pathetic reason
we made God an anthromorph,
that someone would miss us when
we had ourselves to miss,
selves we never put together,
never realized assorted parts,
prohibitively expensive,
obsolete at birth, parts
whose clumsy names deluded us,
damned us with religions
and the pretense of knowledge
whereas we would miss nothing
had we pursued unknowing.

What Luciano said

See that everybody gets what they want;
all I want is everything else.
That's what Luciano said in my dream,
and I immediately set about looking
for how it might be playing out
when I noticed dandelions cavorting
in the warmth of waste, and I knew
they're my salad, my else, and my due.

Skirt disappearing behind a door

I've never wanted to disturb the world
or even move the air around me much.

It didn't seem appropriate for a visitor
who didn't plan to stay very long.

I felt that I had lost something
and searched each face for it.

Occasionally there would be a flash,
the scent of a memory, a murmur,

but then awareness would become a skirt
disappearing behind a closing door.

I accepted that as normalcy
only to wake up in old age

to see my life as an act of respect,
the gesture of a distant, beckoning queen.

The death of me to say

I can't remember doing something so bad with them
that they won't clean up, so I call them second hands,
my first having washed themselves of this world,
second hands that have dirty work to do, work
that should have been done when I walked straight,
but I didn't talk straight and I succumbed
to the wiles of my imagination. I took the moment
for a gnat in the pupil of my eye instead of a tear.
I can't go on. I can't do the crying I refused to do.
Too late for that. But I can scrawl in honest grit
the words I thought would be the death of me to say.

Deuteronomy 23:2

Deuteronomy 23:2

*No one born of a forbidden union may enter the assembly of the Lord.
Even to the tenth generation, none of his descendants...*

It took a wile or two and even then
it was hard to get a mechanic's purchase
on bastardy as transfiguration, but when he did
he emerged from the King James whole,
not belonging to anyone, not longing
to enter into the conjugation of one damned thing,
a rogue cell in the body politic, an anarchist
who thought of flags as diapers.

Glorious bastardy, sinistral, sinister,
a threat to the authorized version of events,
a backwards storyteller, nonsense jabberer,
on the outs, mooning insiders through their thermopains.
But it wasn't easy, it was a sandhogger's job
clearing the tunnel between the eye and the brain,
and another kind of job convincing the brain
to live with the evidence.

No berserker in its maze

I don't grasp the significance of anything,
but occasionally its fragrance makes me tipsy.
I'm not unstrung by what eludes me,
I'm usually its collaborator,
no berserker in its maze.
I'm about unknowing and unbelonging,
looking out and looking in, but not being right
of getting over on or being accepted
owing to the terrible by whom? Not about grasping
or holding on or falling from a height or ascending,
not about being about or even enjoying the discourse.
What does significance have to do with pronouns?
All I have to do is done until it comes back.
I exist to welcome it with open arms.

Which butterfly

You thought you had something to prove to them,
it wasn't medicine enough for either of you.
They took the easy way out, they died
without surrendering their names
to the sea, leaving arrangements
to their pro forma facsimiles.
But you took to examining rotting clapboard,
to protecting buttercups and dandelions from the blade,
and to imagining yourself floating away in a soapy bubble
blown by a child on a stoop, and all that remains to do
is to select the child, or perhaps merely to wait to see
which butterfly in Mexico engineers the event.

Dancing the pale

Compass rose and dartboard aim
at going, getting, coming to some there
to possess therein,
and because they embody,
embrace, circularity, enclosure, containment,
like amphorae,
and worship wherein,
numbers always threaten to break out,
autistic numbers shuddering
at touch, despising their imprisonment,
the idea of there being there,
preferring infinity, redefining light.

Numbers don't patrol parameters,
or serve the state or fear the cold,
they're civilly disobedient,
they don't trade in glamor or allure,
but they won't turn you into castrati
in the middle of the night.

What we might call betrayals,
the conspiracies we bemoan,
are the ecstasies of creatures
sitting on our roofs at night.

We think they wear our uniforms,
but they're protecting us from their nakedness;
it is too bright.

Hurt

Everything I eat hurts,
and in the galaxy between my ears
mercury's always in retrograde.
I'd put this down to old age,
but memory wouldn't let me get away with it.
It's my birthright, a constant call to duty,
the duty of staring what's harmful
in the face until one of us withers.
We must attend each other's funerals
and spend our lives contriving
how that must be possible.

Diet of whales

Hot truck
maladjusted mirror
all kinds of other shit to contend with
no wonder language doesn't suit me anymore
poor damned substitute for a look

I wish all the words gone to hell had tasted like anchovies
wound around capers

then perhaps we would
have thought twice about serving them
to those we said we loved
and we might look as if
we'd tasted them going down

Apologies, anchovy,
a caper's not your pearl
and with a sop of bread you help me
remember when I was the diet of whales

Presumption of dandelions

Another damned winner to celebrate
while we poison dandelions
and hardly know how to honor daffodils.
Never mind the Lenten rose breaking through the snow,
we have contests to enter, conferences to go.
Never mind how much we overlook
to get over on, how avid to sell less
than we're given free. Never mind
the shriveling of sensibility like papier maché
on a twisted wire, we have a cup to receive,
a gavel to pass, certificates of excellence
to crow about, a blurb to publish, a critique
to fart in the face of roses. How dare clover
spot our excellent lawns, plaintain divert golf balls,
how dare dark matter presume on all that we make light?

Death-dancing

Are we here?
Do you notice us?
Are we annoying?
Don't you understand
how much we need you
to be our audience if only
to convince you that you are
our chrysalises?
We intend
to leave you behind
choking in our commotion.
Be grateful that we didn't ask you
to do a death dance for us,
and that little sketch
you're making of our strut,
choke on it.
We don't wish you quiet people well.

Watching the furies slip by

Let me worry for you,
worry these things to emerald and gold
let me be your undoing, your unknowing,
and you, having nowhere to be,
always becoming
will watch the furies slip by
in convoy at night.

Was it a dream?

I know I wrote that poem,
its letters hoisting signals,
but now they've deserted the page.
and the page looks like the abandoned fort
in *Beau Geste*, manned by the dead.

The letters formed ships, the ships
sailed off the flat earth, and when I woke
I searched my notebooks
but could not find that fleet and now
I'm wondering if what I remember
wasn't meant to be said.

And of a poem that isn't meant to be said,
fort meant to be overrun, a port
made to be set out from but not returned to
what is safe to say, what will not betray
the integrity of a dream that went to lengths
to become reality and then erased itself
like a Sufi's trail?

Was it a beau geste,
a beau geste in what cause, saying
some things are their own end
and it is not necessary to wake from them
or attempt to share them,
not necessary and perhaps a betrayal?
I don't know, I don't know how
to respect unknowing, but I'm learning.

Wary greetings

It doesn't take long to become a stranger
considering our wont to withdraw
and the mathematical probability is
we reconsider to hone ourselves
but the curtain blowing in the blasted window,
the vacant eye, the lunar indifference
in once warm faces is hard to survive
and some of us don't although I think we hang
those wary greetings out to dry
in the withering sun of our inquiries.

We are strangers even to our fondest memories
and they have conflated themselves and learned
to ambush what our eyes first saw
on its journey to the brain. Memories become
guerrillas fighting for a cause that seems
to have originated on an alien planet.
We are not so much archaeologists
as naturalists
or we join them in their conspiracies and are lost
to comrades who move on.

Not since Brooklyn

Did I ever want a home to miss?
Not since Brooklyn and then I didn't know how to miss.
I arrived homesick,
unwilling to go on.
After Brooklyn
no face promised to be familiar long,
no place could be trusted
to be there when I got back,
and the adverb there
was a shed in the rain.
I came to give up the prize,
not to win it and make myself at home,
but if I had to choose a home I hankered
for curtains stirring in rotten windows,
I hankered to ignite and cast light.

Dragons kinder

A day of things gone wrong,
sore foot, broken camera,
words that abandon pages, shops
that have moved away don't compare
to being born with antennae
where my penis should have been,
with a third eye for a heart and a brain
more like a Viking funeral ship
than algorithms.
Nothing computes,
so I'm loading the numerals in the hold
and setting out to consort with dragons
kinder than the fakes I knew.

Other sleeplessness to do

Let me be the sleepless one.
I don't need as much as you,
don't want as much as you,
do want to unfold to you,
always wanted to. Sleep
unsure of anything but that you fell asleep
and may wake up in my arms
if you climb the rope of dreams,
and if you fall it won't be
the first time I loitered foolishly.
I won't fish your body out,
I have other sleeplessness to do
and unfolding if not to you.
Let me do the worrying too.
I'm not the one who needs to wake,
but I am one with you.

The drowning

Any minute that's something to get through
shows up later as bones to trip on.
Can't you hear him saying who
drowned while you took time to grow up,
too much time if you ask me
but you didn't and now you hear him saying
why didn't you give me your hand, you
whose hair I smoothed in your sleep?
Why?

What I'm doing in this room

Words like *it, there* and *here* I've been unable to banish.
Friends in high places, you know. So I've become pregnant
with a world of my own, humming into existence
a spinning reverie. Don't ask me who the father is,
virgin births are more common than you think,
but you must bear intense light, burn previous shadows away
to cast a new one that becomes the world
as the others creep into the cracks in the floor
where you stand bringing the moon up while your other hand
attends to the banishment of pretense. Nothing's here,
there is myth, and it is a way of saying pardon me
for thinking I might cast my own world on the grass
and walk barefoot in its dew to a dispensation
I didn't have to borrow from you.

Savage in your compassion

You you you ululating, galaxies of remembrances,
explain why I sit back to walls in cafés of other worlds
with their platelets of tables tablets templates tablatures,
lying to shapeshifting emissaries
about what I do and do not see,
assuring them of my complete attention while
bestiaries and aviaries of where I have been riot
behind the wall. Treaty upon entreaty,
one imposter to another imposing calm, pretending all is well
assuring them our ghostly luggage is resolved and put away
but knowing we are stopgap measures, chaos boarded up,
left behind, looting in the streets, opportunity spurned
because we had lives to live in clearings up ahead.

To disdain the soaking woods for the clearing is the peril
of forgetting why you live, a grabber's game,
a collector's loss. You can see in the dark and pass through walls
but you must consent to the poisons of the moment
and not pretend you have forgotten who you have been,
that you you you ululating in savage dress, consent
to terror and awake with its teeth strung around your neck,
savage in your compassion for the lowliest event,
for butterflies alighting in a muddy ditch to fire up
a marvelous machine, a solution to the insoluble, a cure
for waking up afraid, for being unable to hold up the wall
in this new café. Ask what is the role of luck.
Are you listening?

Jerusalem

The past is not my eminent domain,
it was taken by corsairs to Tripoli
or removed by Turks to Istanbul
or reinstalled by Lake Titicaca,
taken after vespers, chalices,
women and children gone,
and I followed the ley line on
to Jerusalem where I wept,
my freedom to be stripped
of the delusion that I own
what I experience.

Domain's as evil as a name;
neither belongs to us; they're sticks
picked up to help us manage hard terrain.
How can we complain of having no wings
hot as we are for such pretentious luggage?
Jerusalem's where we go to divest our business interests,
otherwise we haven't got a prayer.

Black hole

Do nothing
and when the occasion arises
do nothing again
until the phantom face
appears in the knothole
of time and bares its teeth
or purses its lips and then
do not what mind reasons
but what heart wants
and if you fall and are shaken
out of orbit fall in grace
into the arms of another galaxy.
Do nothing, be
the awful mass of mattter
to which moments tumble.

Waters rising

I was born for you to taste me.
The city undertook its destiny
to be intersected by ships
once she said it, and she became
Thalassa. What possessed her
to say such a thing to a broken man
on a park bench on an August day
when she should have skated by?
Economies collapse for lesser reasons.
She should have gone home and painted her nails
or masturbated or broken someone's heart,
but the words fell out of her mouth,
an unassisted orgasm, and she stood
frozen in an unfathomable gaze,
the odors of pretzels and dirty-water dogs
locked outside the project
of two improbables discovering
nothing natural about the world.

Gentrification

The matter with it is who lives in it
and what matters to them.
That's the matter with us
and all our renovations
can't scrub out or paint over
the witness of our eyes or the reluctance of our doors
to admit the majority of inquirers.

The ghosts of our amenities
are circuit-breakers saving us from fire
always present in the walls.
We are our outages and only another poem
is the back-up generator that makes the dark a pale
of this encampment.
We are your green screens, you are paint.

Eleven lines

They're often dead by the time their intentions become clear,
or you are. To whom is this clarity due—
some unknown species, someone's bud opening
to scent the night air of a distant planet?
I don't know and this unknowing is grandeur enough
to bear my funeral boat out beyond the flares
of an acquisitive society to the terrible calm
where secrets belly up and there is no chagrin.
There is no time for sorrow because there is no time;
elation is an entry point to where I don't know
and, unknowing, I'm not human anymore.

Beyond Montauk

Without the fuss and bother of giving a damn

And then near the end of my life I become the sort of man
I wanted to be without the fuss and bother of giving a damn.
My dreams begin to haunt my face.
My moral compass case cracks
creating a terrarium of odd fungi
in which to wander as a mite.
I know why moss hides,
what long shadows mean, so I
make it through to have my brow smoothed
in the elf queen's house
and my soul tucked in.
True north between my toes, I improvised
even though it let night creatures in.
I was curious and grew back limbs,
took the counsel of bums and infuriated
whoever was pleased to write me off
and boogie on my misfortunes.
They will never touch the elf queen's heart,
practical and acquisitive as they are;
they failed the test of adoration,
they were in awe not of cracks in walls
but foolish possibilities held out to them.
They treasured nonsense not, gibberish
they eschewed, they therefore spoke such sense
they could not hear the fairy whistles
calling them off the bristly field, and as for sight
they saw with such acuity they could not see

their elemental company, and so it was by default
they achieved their low ambitions, while I
chose not to die but disappear.

If you can't bring yourself

Don't come if you can't bring yourself
or can't bring yourself to bear
the savage looks of the fey gathered here,
don't come splattering cheap good will,
bling on us and fester of wounds.
Bring that wan self screwed by dreams
before you look in the mirror, before
you smooth your face in expectation
of what the day may bring, bring
the betrayed child to my home, insist
that I not patronize him, and I won't.
That is my promise to you if you dare
to come to, come to yourself before arriving.

To make crows laugh

The world teems with *theres* more real than *here*.
Here is quicksand, quagmire, graves opening. Here
is what we imagine it, enticing,
letters from a friend, a cornucopia
of first times. There! An accomplishment,
a place that can be left with honor,
no hanging on the doorknob, no protestation
of undying love but love taken with you.
Where *there* is, something follows, but *here*
each action flows backward leaving
only condoms, *here* is a rebar
in a pedestal, life is self-worship, thought
is a stand, and yet there is no way to go *there*
except to swim in this quarry and drown,
this particular quarry, while friends give accounts of you
that make crows laugh and aspens tinkle.

The painting

I exist to pester the calm of your face.

But you no longer exist.

I exist more than when I had an address.
Now I am an unassailable moment
without yesterday or tomorrow.
I have no baggage, no et cetera,
nothing to distract you but a perfect stare.

What do I do?

I don't care. More important, why should you?

Bewilderness

she hears what he hums to himself
and knows there is something divine
in the heart of horror

he has the face of a hawk
and its merciless eyes
but the melody ravishes her

in hubbub and silence she sees
the truth about angels,
they would need halos

or upraised hands
if the painters got them right,
they would terrify us

with reassurances
that in this bewilderness
we must love what we deny

Hospital earth

Can we walk around?

His wounds are giant screwholes
by which we hold down our grief.

We are his bronze plaques
saying tragically usual things.

Can we walk around
to assure ourselves life is going on
if only in a murmur of green scrubs?

Words rifle into our granite minds,
janitors will polish us at night
with solvent dreams,
gurneys will rush past bearing
the crashes of civilizations
and we will grieve more than relatives
because we have had time for terror
to sink in, its pink hue announcing
the costliness of another day.

Can we walk around,
buy gewgaws in the gift shop,
slug a machine, slurp coffee
and listen to the wind arguing
with canopies while instruments
inside measure the varying degrees
of hopelessness and shifts change
the greater hopelessness of going home?

Can we walk around
to work the corrosion out of our bones,
to look in on the casualties of war
and infamous diplomacies
that bring the earth to this hospital
of emergency operations
to repair the heart at cost of the soul?

Who is dead,
whose death awoke us past midnight
and brought us here in an ambulance
of schadenfreude because it's not us,
not yet, so we can celebrate,
grim-faced as we are,
with another war?

Who is dead?
That is why we walk around to see,
to understand why we are here,
not sleeping in our beds
but pretending we know what to do,
how to grieve, who to grieve, when
all we know is how to bolt ourselves in
against demons riding hurricanes
and calling themselves our friends.

Can we walk around
to shake ourselves from this dream?

Witch's skirt

Size and shape lie in ruins,
their names may well be runes.
He used to know square from circle,
oval from aught, height, width, depth,
even their uses, but the moon
pulls their tides out. Gravity
goes up in smoke. Measure
seems a presumption. Place
a melting chunk of ice. Panic
turns to ecstasy. Weight
is temporary inconvenience.
He has become a rune sewn
into a witch's skirt.

As if Hopper

So you would do this until you stop,
which might or might not be the end,
as if you'd been arrested, or is it detained,
and told the magistrate wasn't coming
until the truce was signed on Sirius,
but what were you doing, could it be explained,
was it a matter of apertures and speeds
or perhaps the matter with them? In any case,
the food isn't bad and as far as you know
you're not being charged with a criminal offense,
and if you'd been living inoffensively
you wouldn't be worth charging with anything,
so take heart, if that's what you have left,
do a little gardening, draw a picture,
discover your hidden talent for emptiness,
as if Hopper once had arrested you.

Bird-watching

When you fall out is it as hard
as when you fell out then—
the hundred then and theres,
—street corners and phone booths
(remember them?) with their directories?
I don't think so, no, not as hard,
maybe even more a triumph,
small as a cough drop,
than a disappointment.
Not as hard or long a fall,
but it's thrilling,
more like a bungee jump
than a roller coaster
to know I found something out,
not an epiphany exactly,
more like adding to a life list,
a feat of identification,
not to celebrate with another drink
or anything as adolescent,
but to take into account
as if it would outlast me
and is meanwhile
something I can endure.

To hang on the doorknob

What should I wear—
panties, scarf, sweater?
Better it should come off in my hand.
I could give it to a child
as I head down the street
to erasure in the rain.

No sense hanging around
in the vague hope my hosts
will like me any better
than my mother did,
not when the question is
do I like them any better
than I liked her.

I'm not going to linger
on anybody's doorknob.
I know what that's about,
smelly opprobrium, spite,
disgrace of having to admit
I was like the bastards after all.

Sorting

Whatever we do we're covering
something else we do
and the roar of such machineries
deafens us to each other's pleas
for mercy from our desires.

How long before this melts the ice caps
and drowns the cities where we've come
not to love but to acquire
the whims of our imaginings,
how long before we drown in them?

So little we cannot give each other
and yet the blue earth to withhold,
so little we can conceal and yet
what glee concealing it, so much
we ought to be sorting in the light.

Burnt stick

Stuff my shirt with belief,
burn it in the wind,
I will watch the tatters fly,
I will see myself away,
and what is left, a burnt stick,
will mark the trail
of those I'd like to have been.

What more had I forgotten?

Toward the end of it all I became concerned with shafts of light
as if my ancestors were arriving and I had not completed
the prescribed preparations for them. I had forgotten them.
What more had I forgotten? Could I remember in time
where to stand and what to do? I was optimistic if only
because I didn't want anything more than to prepare.

There is already nothing more to say, so that is not a problem,
I am merely cutting the stems of words so they can drink
to bloom another day. I am surveying new Nazca lines
not to bring strange aircraft down or pray to gods
but to propose a few equations and then invite
my harem of dead idiots to solve them.

Letter to name withheld

I'm trying to draw your silence,
its arabesques and washes, the way
the pencil navigates the paper's thread,
the elongated calculations and hints
of relentless travel in bed. Color
would be as detrimental as a name.
To confuse the interrupted line
with ellipses would be my undoing
as much as yours. I must make sure
each line arrives in a hidden place,
and there its profane rites,
the gods' suggestions, are ignored
at peril. That peril as much as silence
is what I'm after, what you better hope
I never send, what you've given away.

I would like to wake in a formal garden

butterflies in a silver sea at my feet.
If you wish this for me I will remember you.
Let us make no further plans. Developments
will be the consequence of butterflies,
names will turn to pollen,
and I will walk away.

No maze, I will be done with that,
but I would like an arboretum to shelter in
when thunder shakes the ground and lightning
limns the true shape of ideas. I will fade
and fall apart, I will not intrude or possess.
After a long while smiling in the evening
I will walk away.

Nothing will ever be true again,
or false, and whatever I understood
will become light taking its time
to arrive upon the face of one
who seeing me across the street
will remember a great bonfire
before doubts closed in.

Beyond Montauk

Don't look back is like saying look,
I'm tightrope walking, thinking
don't look too far ahead, stop
this chasm from BC to AD is
more alluring than the other side.

Time stopped when I kissed Mary Corbett.

The wire throbbed and nothing good
would ever happen again in spite
of rosy promises, even those I believed,
nothing good because the sweetness of her breath
opened my pores to true intent
and nothing could shut them to storms,
nothing good because pretense
would never come easy again.

We should have gone on to Babylon
to see a movie, not swim
in each other's eyes.

                                  After my death,
which ought to have been a beginning
of something more than Amityville,
all I wanted to be was one
with how it happens, the music
and the mathematics of it.
                                I wanted
not to want at all, beyond Montauk.

Dumping the apartment

Dumping the apartment

If I dump this apartment
with all its apart-ments while
entertaining a sore throat
it may prevent an earthquake
or knock a planet out of orbit.

Scientists might scoff,
but they're pigeonholers
& incident reporters
while I'm a co-operator
of the temporarily unexplained,
conspirator with butterflies
& people with pentaquarks
in their heads, pinholes for eyes
casting shadow plays in boxes.

Shedding clothes is easier
than our names.   A good start
is ripping up baggage claims—
an essay on the sovereignty of light.

I'll miss everything about the place,
especially picking up nostalgia,
the obsequiousness of doormen,
all that couldn't substitute for love,
views & inconsiderate neighbors,
implacable as family, native
compared to the ways I'm foreign.

I've missed bad places before,
settled in the Dachaus of the mind
& learned to love the guards.

That's enough of that,
we'll talk about it some other time.

Let gargoyles rest,
pretensions be left behind.
Let roof gardens cook,
elevators break down,
assessments go up,
balconies come down.

Let the glyphs in the street
become the dead sea scrolls,
the old testament to which we hark back
because the new one is too hard, too bright
& all too gaily fitted out
to sail melted glaciers like
a trading ship in a bottle.

If I sail this apartment
with its hold of oppugnants
in the rogue vortices & squalls
of my inmost fears, how
should I explain this mutiny,
or better yet, to whom?

My life hasn't spoken for itself;
can that be left behind?

www.ingramcontent.com/pod-product-compliance
Lightning Source LLC
LaVergne TN
LVHW041547070426
835507LV00011B/964